FOCUS GROUPS

The original text for this publication was produced by the Personnel
Communication Unit, BT, on behalf of

The Organisational Development Unit
BT Centre
81 Newgate Street
London EC1A 7AJ

FOCUS GROUPS

INVOLVING EMPLOYEES CREATIVELY TO INFLUENCE DECISIONS

Original text written by BT Organisational Development

The Industrial Society

First published in 1997 by
The Industrial Society
Robert Hyde House
48 Bryanston Square
London W1H 7LN
Telephone: 0171–262 2401

Original © British Telecommunications plc 1996
Additional text © The Industrial Society 1996
Typographical arrangement © The Industrial Society 1996

ISBN 185835 873 6

British Library Cataloguing-in-Publication Data.
A catalogue record for this book is available from the
British Library

Typeset by: Gilbert Composing Services
Printed by: Lavenham
Cover design: Form Design

Text illustrations: Martin Shovel

CONTENTS

SECTION 1: ABOUT FOCUS GROUPS   1
What they are and when to use them; comparisons with other
research methodologies; Omnibus Focus Groups.

SECTION 2: PLANNING   9
Commissioning the research; matching proposals to needs;
choosing the participants.

SECTION 3: PREPARATION   21
Designing the programme; finding participants and making
arrangements for the day.

SECTION 4: RUNNING THE GROUPS   35
Tasks of the moderator and scribe; questioning and listening
techniques; dealing with tricky situations.

SECTION 5: THE FINDINGS   49
Writing the report; feedback to interested parties.

SECTION 6: REVIEW OF THE RESEARCH   59
The importance of validation and evaluation.

SECTION 7: USEFUL INFORMATION   63
Checklist; registration of data; current research year plan.

APPENDICES: Viewpoint BT Case Studies
1. The Employee Handbook   69
2. Further Investigation of Employee Attitude Data   70
3. Employees' Evening   71

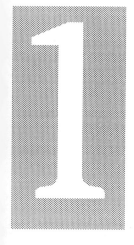

ABOUT FOCUS GROUPS

WHAT IS A FOCUS GROUP?

A focus group is a method for getting people to think creatively and to share openly their opinions about a chosen topic.

It helps managers to understand the opinions of their people and how these should influence strategy, policy and the implementation of policy.

The method involves identifying people who are in some way affected by, or interested in, the subject concerned, and bringing a group of them together in a relaxed environment to discuss some of the issues involved.

APPLICATIONS

Focus groups can help to:

- identify the positive and negative features of situations;

- anticipate the thoughts, feelings and actions of people when planning new initiatives;

- reveal preferences for, or against, alternatives being considered;

- test out reactions to new policies, products and services before they are introduced;

- identify potential barriers to implementation and look for creative ways to overcome them;

- obtain feedback about programmes during roll-out so that subsequent stages can be adjusted if necessary;

- evaluate activity once completed; learn lessons for future improvement;

- improve employee involvement and participation in company decision making; identify issues for inclusion in quantitative research (e.g. survey design);

- help to explain the reasons behind quantitative research findings.

Focus group research can play a part, at virtually any stage, in the introduction of a product or service. In designing the focus group it is important to be clear about the purpose of that particular phase of data collection.

CHARACTERISTICS

Focus groups have the following attributes:

Non directive: There is a certain amount of freedom for the discussion to follow its own direction and generate unexpected, but potentially useful ideas;

Safe conditions: The success of a focus group depends on creating the kind of environment in which people feel physically and emotionally comfortable, and are willing to share their views honestly and without fear of retribution;

Internal dynamics: The stimulus for the discussion is generated internally within the group, not just by the questioner; people respond to one another and the method exploits these interactions;

Creativity: Were it not for a creative component the focus group might better be described as a group interview. The method allows for people to develop ideas as they go along, building on the views expressed by others. Participants are encouraged to think laterally and suggest improvements rather than passively accepting the status quo;

Depth: Focus groups are intended to delve beneath the surface, to explore people's feelings and probe their motives; to seek root causes rather than symptoms.

WHO SHOULD USE FOCUS GROUPS?

If you are faced with the need to understand a situation for example, the issues behind your employee survey results, you may find that certain features of the focus group approach are useful when involving your people in discussion.

If you support line managers in developing the organization, focus groups can provide a useful way of collecting data on behalf of clients and feeding it back in an absorbing and accessible way.

If you are a professional researcher, focus groups will be an essential part of your armoury of techniques for answering clients' enquiries, particularly when used in conjunction with other complementary methods.

There is a note of caution though: as those who regularly use focus groups will be only too aware, there are numerous pitfalls and the approach can easily be discredited by thoughtless and unprofessional application.

BENEFITS

Although the primary aim of focus group research is to collect data to enhance action planning and bring about change, there may be significant side benefits:

- focus groups are a learning environment that can help people tackle problem solving and can make them aware of people management issues;

- focus groups permit people to express their feelings and opinions in depth and at length, which can have a cathartic effect, a feeling of having 'got it off my chest';

- focus groups bring people from different work environments together for a common activity and help to reinforce teamworking across the organisation;

- focus groups are a social activity, allowing people to interact with others and share experiences;

- focus groups can help to engender a sense of involvement and participation among those who take part and may be seen by others as a visible demonstration that the company is willing to listen to employee concerns;

- those running focus groups have been known to gain from them in the following ways:
  - social satisfaction from contact with those 'at the sharp end';
  - kudos from being regarded as the visiting expert; enhanced understanding of the issues discussed;
  - a sense of having contributed to a worthwhile activity.

OTHER METHODS OF DATA COLLECTION

Compared to other methods of data collection, focus groups are notable for their potential to yield rich, qualitative information that can be presented in a lively way (for example, by using direct quotes). However, they are relatively resource intensive, require sensitive handling for maximum benefit and are unsuited to the collection of large amounts of quantitative data.

While it is impossible to be definitive, the table on the next page attempts to summarize the pros and cons of focus groups in comparison with some other research methods.

Focus Groups Compared With Other Research Methodologies

Focus groups ——————————————————————————————————————┐
Postal questionnaire ——————————————————————————————┐ │
Telephone interview (structured) ————————————————┐ │ │
Face-to-face interviews (semi-structured) ———┐ │ │ │

	Focus groups	Postal questionnaire	Telephone interview (structured)	Face-to-face interviews (semi-structured)
Design expertise required	H	H	H	H
Involvement/exposure for client	M	M	L	M
Time/effort to set up	H	M	H	H
Interviewer/administrator skill	H	M	L	H
Detachment/objectivity of researcher	L	M	H	L
Breadth of issues that can be covered	L	M	H	L
Depth/flexibility of questioning	H	M	L	H
Involvement/interest for participants	H	M	L	H
Learning/development for participants	M	L	L	H
Anonymity for participants	H	H	H	M
Cost/time per participant	H	M	L	M
Ease of analysis and interpretation	M	H	H	L
Meaningful/relevant results	H	M	L	H
Credibility of method with client	M	M	H	M
Generalisation of data	L	M	H	L

H = High   M = Medium   L = Low

OMNIBUS FOCUS GROUPS

'Omnibus' surveys are surveys which are carried out regularly and on an ongoing basis. Relevant or key issues can then be surveyed as they arise by 'slotting' them into the existing survey framework.

ADVANTAGES OF OMNIBUS SURVEYS

By running a regular survey, administration costs can be minimised. It is also usually possible to insert questions or issues at quite short notice, thus ensuring quick feed-back.

A regular planned programme of focus groups provides an opportunity for clients to commission slots within a pre-planned programme rather than having to set up groups from scratch.

Different people participate in the different focus groups, which should be run by trained moderators or facilitators.

STRUCTURE

The structure of each group session is usually along the following lines:

- 'top-of-the-mind' issues raised by participants;
- two client-specified issues (company-wide);
- regular culture measure (e.g. employee satisfaction);
- process review.

LIMITATIONS

Omnibus focus groups are company-wide, untargeted in the selection of participants, and therefore unlikely to be suitable for research that seeks to:

- concentrate on particular categories of people (for example, customers of an internal service);

- explore issues of relevance only to certain parts of the organisation.

PLANNING

COMMISSIONING THE RESEARCH

As the organizer/designer of a focus group research project, you will have to make an early decision on who to commission to do the fieldwork and reporting. Should it be carried out by the department requiring the information, by some other specialist unit within your organisation, or by external consultants? Here are some of the advantages and disadvantages of each which you might like to consider.

OWN UNIT

Pros	Cons
In depth knowledge of product/subject	Discussion can easily turn into a debate with focus group moderator
Familiar with background, context and organisation	Results may be perceived as biased if they reflect well on unit concerned
Well able to deliver improvements based on research findings	Emotional involvement in topic may influence participants
Participants feel that they have direct access to those who count	May already have desired outcome in mind and overlook alternatives
Researchers able to deal with questions raised by participants	May lack research skills and experience
Better awareness of resource requirements and hence appreciation for value of work undertaken	May not have sufficient time or resources
Involvement may lead to a high commitment to act on results	Analysis may be too parochial (interpreting all data in terms of work of own unit only)

INTERNAL SPECIALIST

Pros	*Cons*
Knows company can appreciate client's problems	Client may have to make a case for specialist help
Well placed to tap into related research efforts and exploit established networks	Time needed to explain requirements to a third party
No external costs	Objectivity may be coloured by organisation's cultural norms
Specialist expertise and experience available	Knowledge of other organisation and external practice may be limited
Relatively impartial and objective	
Able to offer anonymity to participants	
Will take wider view when interpreting results	
Will ensure good practice is followed	

EXTERNAL CONSULTANTS

Pros	Cons
Objective: not absorbed into organisation's culture	Unknown quantity: need to check credentials
Perceived as more professional	Report may concentrate on less useful areas
Will impress participants	Will require project management
Low pay costs	High non-pay costs
Viewed as impartial	Unfamiliar with organisation's people/structure
Independent viewpoint	May not be fully aware of issues and may misinterpret data
Free of politics of situation	Participants may be suspicious of outsiders
	Commercially driven

DEFINING RESEARCH NEEDS

Whether planning the research yourself, using a specialist group within your organisation or commissioning an outside agency, it is essential to begin by developing a clear statement of research requirements.

The client on behalf of whom you are organising the research programme may be your own unit or another department. In either case, you may find that your client has no more than a vague notion that some sort of research is desirable. In the worst case, the client may be driven by some external requirement to collect data, rather than a personal interest in the findings.

By clearly defining what is required you will ensure that research needs dictate the methodology rather than vice versa. Since it is not unusual for these needs to change during the period of data collection, it is also important that the statement of requirements should be reviewed on a regular basis.

THE RESEARCH BRIEF

Before a sensible methodology can be proposed, the client may need to specify the following:

- background and objectives of the research;

- description of the population of interest (such as customers in certain age groups, organisation types or internal customers in particular functions such as front-line staff, delivery etc.).

- type of research envisaged (tentative at this stage);

- question areas to be covered;
- type of output expected (for example, a written report);
- the intended use of the findings;
- a realistic timetable;
- the budget.

THE RESEARCH PROPOSAL

In response to the brief, your research proposal should be produced and should include:

- a statement of objectives;
- a description of how the research will be done:
  - the sample;
  - the fieldwork;
  - an outline of the focus group structure;
  - administration roles and responsibilities;
  - employee communications and feedback;
- the rationale for the suggested methodology;
- proposals for handling the data;
- proposals for reporting the results;
- process for initiating change based on findings;
- research timetable;
- costs.

FURTHER CLARIFICATION

In relation to the above, it is advisable to clarify the following points with the client at the planning stage:

- what interpretation the client would put on various possible findings;
- how the client would respond in each instance;
- what action the client would then take;
- how the client would communicate this to participants.

The exact mechanisms for the feedback of findings and outcomes to participants and other interested parties (see Section 5) should also be agreed with the client at this stage.

CHOOSING THE PARTICIPANTS

NUMBER OF GROUPS REQUIRED

Unlike questionnaire surveys, the scale of the research tends to be a matter of professional judgement, rather than statistical calculation. The strengths of the focus group are depth, flexibility and creativity, rather than representativeness and statistical validity.

Practical experience suggests a high level of information gain in the first few groups, tailing off rapidly thereafter. As few as half a dozen strategically placed groups can be effective in identifying the main concerns. Even one or two sessions can be helpful during the early stages in a project, or for dealing with small scale problems.

If you are concerned that certain categories of participant should be represented, it would be advisable to ensure that at least one or two of each are invited to every group. One approach is to identify the factors that seem likely to influence opinions on the issue in question, then present these in the form of a matrix, for example:

	Leaving Organization		*Staying With Organization*	
	Male	*Female*	*Male*	*Female*
Urban				
Rural				

By including participants in every cell you can help to guarantee that all the relevant groups are represented. In general, a sample that is structured in this way is more likely to be representative than one that is completely random.

It is worth noting that there are rarely variations between different sub-populations (for example, divisions, functions, grades) and that the headline issues tend to appear fairly early on and change only marginally thereafter. However, the credibility of the findings with the client is a valid consideration and if holding a greater number of groups helps to secure this then it may be worthwhile.

Also relevant is the finding that focus groups can serve purposes other than straightforward data gathering, for example, opportunities to exchange ideas within the group, employee involvement and participation, and cathartic expression. These additional effects might suggest a larger scale of activity than indicated by information needs alone.

SELECTING THE SAMPLE

Normally, the best approach, regardless of protocol or practicalities, would be to draw a random sample from payroll or personnel records and contact participants directly to invite them to take part. At this point, real life starts to intervene in the shape of the following:

- there may not be a single, centrally held list from which the sample base can be identified;

- even when names are available, contact details may be hard to get hold of;

- there may be local conventions to observe, like agreeing a person's release with the relevant line

manager before contacting the individual
concerned;

- operational requirements or work arrangements
  make it hard for people to attend at
  certain times;

- it may not be convenient and/or people may not
  be willing or able to travel to and from the focus
  group location;

- the cost of attending may be a barrier, especially if
  local travel and subsistence budgets are already
  stretched.

In many instances it is more practical to sample clusters of
people from particular locations or organisational units,
rather than spread across the organisation as a whole. The
downside of this is that too much reliance on such 'samples
of convenience' can result in the same people being
included time after time.

For organisation-wide initiatives some local co-
ordination is almost inevitably going to be required and it
may be possible to utilise cross functional networks for this
purpose. Understandably, requests for support at short
notice should be avoided if at all possible.

One option always worth checking out is whether there
are any existing groups or panels onto which the current
research could 'piggy back'.

The important thing is to have a clear sampling strategy
and to understand the pros and cons of the approach
chosen. Specialist advice may be required on the
implications of different sampling methods.

PRIOR PUBLICITY

The situation is changing, but people are generally unaccustomed to being asked directly, and without prior notice, to participate in qualitative employee research. Contact made 'out of the blue' may well cause people to suspect the legitimacy and/or motives of the researcher.

In addition, some managers feel uncomfortable releasing their people to participate in focus groups, without some sort of endorsement from a senior figure in their part of the business.

Prior to recruiting participants, a positioning statement may be required. This should be in keeping with the proposed scale of the research so as not to raise unrealistic expectations about the likelihood of being asked to participate.

Exaggerated claims about the degree of endorsement or level of interest displayed by senior figures in the company can be perceived as overkill and have a counter effect, thus detracting from the reputation of employee research generally.

UNION INVOLVEMENT

It is often wise to involve Unions, where they are recognised. Some employees may check with their union representative before agreeing to attend focus groups. It is helpful if the representatives know of the survey and appreciate the use to which the organisation will put it. If representatives are ignorant of the survey or hostile to it they may discourage people from attending. This could potentially lead to skewing the response. In most cases it is sufficient merely to tell the representatives the scope and purpose of the research.

PREPARATION

DESIGNING THE PROGRAMME

It is quite possible to run a focus group with no more preparation than an introduction to create the right atmosphere, and a topic for debate. Thereafter, the moderator applies standard questioning and listening techniques and allows the discussion to find its own direction.

However, there are drawbacks to such a loose approach:

- participants may find the structure dissatisfying as there are no 'anchor points', and the discussion may appear to lack purpose;

- without structured changes of focus, it is hard to maintain interest for the duration of the session;

- discussion may drift from the specified topic;

- the discussion may get bogged down, without a planned change to help move things on;

- important areas may be omitted;

- moderators (and scribes, if used) need to be especially skilful and resourceful to manage the process and record the data;

- because the data may emerge at any time, in any order, and on any facet of the topic, it is difficult to compare and/or combine the output from different groups;

- if more than one moderator is used, it is hard to ensure that they all follow a consistent approach.

A different set of risks arises if the focus group structure is too tightly prescribed/structured, as for example, when all the questions are specified in advance:

- there is little room for error in the design and timing and every eventuality must be catered for in advance;

- the discussion may be constrained from moving into unanticipated, though promising, areas;

- depth and detail of discussion become difficult, possibly resulting in little more than a question-and-answer session;

- if there are no follow up questions, participants may feel that their views are not being properly heard;

- the skills of the moderator (and scribe if used) may be under-utilised;

- there may be excessive duplication in people's responses, with no flexibility to skip sections when this happens.

Most focus groups in organisations are run to a semi-structured format, with a written brief which combines:

- a certain amount of structure, to ensure that different angles of the topic are covered;

- sufficient flexibility for the moderators to adapt their questions in the light of previous answers and to follow up on emergent issues.

GETTING STARTED

Set aside some time at the beginning of the focus group to clarify roles and expectations, and to generally put the group at ease. Do not underestimate the time required for this as it can easily take 15 minutes. Areas to be covered include:

- introducing the moderator (and scribe) and describing their role;
- fire/safety arrangements;
- background to and purpose of the research;
- who has commissioned the research;
- how participants were selected;
- overall structure/timing of the session;
- confidentiality/anonymity;
- voluntary nature of participation;
- thanks for coming;
- participant introductions and collection of biodata;
- any questions.

The moderator should also use this introductory session to set the overall tone for the discussion, emphasising the principles of focus groups:

- they are discussion groups with a research purpose;

- there are no right or wrong answers;

- different views should be respected;

- the moderator is there to steer people through the discussion, not to contribute opinions.

THE CENTRAL CORE

After the introductions, the basis for the focus group design must relate to the client's research needs. The more precisely these have been defined, the more obvious the issues that need to be put to the group and the amount of time that should be spent on each.

Specific areas worthy of exploration may be indicated by other relevant sources, such as:

- previous research (internal and external);

- observational data;

- company records and statistics (for example, financial);

- anecdotal evidence;

- quantitative survey data;

- preliminary one-to-one interviews;

- programme validation data.

For each main question it is usual to generate a list of sub-questions which the focus group moderator can use selectively to probe the participants.

Other factors that may need to be taken into account in structuring the focus group are:

- specific theories concerning the area of enquiry:

for example, known factors affecting motivation at work;

- prior expectations of participants: springing surprises on people is dishonest and asking for trouble, so stick to subject areas and ways of obtaining information that are culturally acceptable;

- time available: do not be overly ambitious in the amount of material included; most people find that the process takes longer in real life than anticipated;

- concentration span of participants: incorporate breaks and changes of task and of direction at regular intervals; try to avoid the material becoming repetitious; two to two-and-a-half hours (including a ten minute break) should be quite enough for most groups;

- the experience and limitations of the moderator: the demands made in terms of task complexity must be within the capabilities of the moderator;

- the size of the group: the larger this is the longer the discussion will generally take and the harder it will be for shy individuals to speak up;

- the sensitivity of the subject matter: do not ask about areas that that embarrass people in front of their colleagues; if these are unavoidable, consider using an alternative method such as individual interviews;

- the designer's own intuition and common sense: although the client may not specify this, it might make sense to collect the information required by encouraging people to give their views under headings such as, say, 'sources of satisfaction', 'sources of dissatisfaction' and 'areas for improvement';

- the logical order of the topic: for example, if considering the effectiveness of a particular business process, it may be worthwhile working through it chronologically from beginning to end;

- the emotional impact on participants: it is advisable to start with a few fairly harmless questions before moving on to more contentious issues.

At every stage in the design, you should keep in mind how the data is to be recorded, summarised and fed back, and the client's likely reactions. For example, there is little value in collected opinions on issues that the client is unwilling or unable to accept or respond to.

    If the client responds best to 'hard information', it may be unwise to spend a lot of time on projective exercises.

INTRODUCING VARIETY

In addition to straightforward questioning, some useful activities that can be built into the programme include:

- voting on a particular issue, and then explaining the reasons for the choices made;

- brainstorming ideas, then reviewing and discussing the list generated;

- prioritizing some given options and then reflecting on how decisions were reached;

- sorting information cards according to a given criteria;

- recalling, describing and considering critical events from personal experience;

- discussing a controversial statement (for example, a declaration of principle about what the organisation expects of its people);

- critiquing specific products (either mock-ups or real-life material);

- commenting on data already collected from other sources (such as a quantitative survey);

- asking people to entertain a fictitious scenario and say what they would do in that situation (for example, 'imagine you were running the company, what would you do about...?');

- performing a creative task (such as painting a picture, storyboarding a video, writing a story) and discussing the output.

The common feature of these activities is that they stimulate people to look at things in new and creative ways, and to bring issues to the surface that might otherwise go unnoticed. Data might be provided not only by what people say, but also by what they do in such circumstances.

Of course, the further away the stimulus is from a neutral question, the more likely it is to influence the response. It is up to the person reporting the focus group output to bear this in mind when interpreting what people say. In general, it is probably wise to stack the more 'exotic' exercises towards the end of the session, to avoid them exerting an undue influence on the session as a whole.

TESTING THE STRUCTURE

Before 'going live', it is critical to pilot the proposed session with a group of friendly volunteers. An observer should monitor the timings and note any hitches as they occur. A detailed review should be held with the participants. One aim is to understand how the session felt for participants and to make improvements accordingly.

It may be possible to carry out the test during a briefing/skills practice session for the focus group moderators and scribes, thus saving time.

CLIENT INVOLVEMENT

It might be tempting to invite the client to design the group process, but there are difficulties with this:

- getting involved in the detail of the group design may distract the client from more important issues, such as how the research should be positioned and how the findings will be used;

- it is difficult for the client, with pet theories and agendas to support, to produce an impartial design;
- the client is unlikely to have the necessary experience and expertise.

Therefore, focus group design is generally best undertaken by specialists who are independent of the commissioning client. Nevertheless, there are advantages in obtaining some degree of involvement by the client (for example to prioritize draft sections according to their importance in the finished product).

At the very least, the client should see the finished design and confirm that it will collect the type of information required.

ADDITIONAL MATERIAL

In addition to designing the structure for the group itself, it is necessary to produce a process for recording and summarizing what has been said. The collection of quantitative data will almost certainly require some sort of proforma to log the information in a consistent format.

If the fieldwork involves co-ordinating a team of people, the following should also be included in the brief:

- background to the research;
- client brief/research proposal;
- procedures for recruiting participants;
- details of publicity/positioning communications;
- participant pre-briefing materials;
- code of conduct;

- specification of requirements for report/ presentation;

- list of useful contacts.

ORGANISING THE FOCUS GROUPS

CONTACTING PARTICIPANTS

Ideally, contact should be made with participants four to six weeks prior to the group being run, though it is recognised that research often has to be set up in much shorter timescales than this.

When making initial contact with potential participants the following points should be stressed:

- who has commissioned the research;

- who is carrying out the research;

- reasons for the research;

- the purpose of the research;

- why the participants have been selected;

- the voluntary nature of participation;

- the confidential nature of the discussion;

- what can be expected during the session;

- length, date, time, location and travel information; person to contact in the event of problems/ queries;

- arrangements made with line manager (where applicable).

To ensure consistency it is best for one individual (posssibly an administrator) to be solely responsible for calling people up and making the arrangements. This should be someone with a good telephone manner who can be persuasive and persistent as it can be a hard slog getting participants, particularly during holiday periods. The administrator must be fully briefed about the research and its objectives, and may find it helpful to have a script for use as an aide memoir.

Proper records should be kept of: who has agreed to take part; who has refused, with reasons (this can be data in itself); and who would like to take part, but cannot make the date given (useful for follow up research). Reliable details will be helpful not only at this stage, but also when it comes to providing feedback to participants after the event.

Once people have agreed to take part, it is more likely they will attend if they have clear, professional documentation. It is advisable to over recruit slightly to allow for drop outs, say ten to twelve recruits to get six to eight participants, this being the ideal number as a rule of thumb.

It is generally desirable for managers and non managers to attend separate groups, as mixed groups can inhibit discussion.

Line relationships within a particular group should also be avoided, and colleagues who normally work closely together should be separated as this can affect the group dynamics.

PHYSICAL CONDITIONS

Venues need to be booked before arranging participants, moderators and scribes.

The environment in which the focus group takes place

can do much to enhance or detract from the quality of the discussion and generally the most conducive conditions will be found away from the normal workplace. However, an on-site discussion may be advantageous if it relates directly to some aspect of that environment (such as use of equipment or work flows).

The ideal room for the discussion should be light, adequately spacious, reasonably quiet, private, and at a comfortable temperature. Interruptions can be prevented by a suitable notice on the door and by diverting any telephones. If groups are being run back-to-back, it may be necessary to arrange waiting facilities for incoming participants.

Other points to check are:

- transport facilities;

- need for a plan of the location/map of environs;

- visual aids equipment;

- security arrangements for entry to the building;

- provision of hospitality;

- whereabouts of toilets and other facilities;

- fire evacuation procedures;

- whether any fire drills or tests of the alarm are planned.

Furniture and participants should be positioned within the room to encourage an informal and relaxed atmosphere in which communication is made easy. Comfortable seats arranged in a horseshoe or broken circle around a low coffee table seem to work well. It is important that participants can easily see and hear one another and do not find the surroundings off-putting or distracting.

The moderator should remain near to the group and maintain a clear view of all the participants. Some small degree of physical separation may be useful to reinforce the moderator's role as an independent and non-participating facilitator. The observer/scribe should be positioned unobtrusively, perhaps a little way from the group (but definitely not hidden!).

RUNNING THE GROUPS

MODERATORS AND SCRIBES

All focus groups are led by a moderator whose functions include the following:

- setting the scene and creating the right atmosphere;
- structuring the session: managing time;
- steering the group through the questions;
- stimulating discussion and involving the participants;
- encouraging relevant ideas to develop;
- clarifying and checking understanding;
- keeping the debate within boundaries;
- protecting the rights and welfare of participants;
- making notes and observations;
- dealing with any issues or queries.

In addition, the moderator may be involved in:

- designing and developing the focus group structure;
- recruiting and inviting participants to attend;

- setting up the groups;

- data analysis and report writing;

- providing feedback to participants.

It is essential in good practice that groups should be supported by a scribe, or note taker; an individual with primary responsibility for observing and recording the verbal and non-verbal behaviour of the group. This requires neutrality, concentration, fast, legible note-taking, and the ability to summarize streams of ideas as they emerge.

The scribe must be prepared to say if a point has been missed or requires clarification, but will otherwise adopt a background role.

Tape-recording is a legitimate method of recording the data without distortion. However, it is not intended to replace the scribe. Although standard in customer research, the approach is less likely to be accepted by employees. The time taken to decipher and transcribe the tape can prevent this being worthwhile, and of course the non-verbal information is lost.

It is important that moderators and scribes understand the extent and limits of their roles and responsibilities, and that they work well together. Indeed it is common for moderators and scribes to agree to reverse roles for successive sessions or parts of a session.

For one person to carry out the two roles simultaneously is demanding and should not be attempted without a good deal of practice and experience. Even then, to allow for this, some concessions may be needed in the design of the focus group structure (for example, increased use of flip-charts for recording information).

QUESTIONING TECHNIQUES

The focus group process relies heavily on flexibility of enquiry. While the initial question in each section may be written into the brief, subsequent prompts may have to be determined on the spot by the focus group moderator, based on the earlier responses.

Questions must be clear and simple, avoiding the use of ambiguous words or confusing sentence construction.

Different types of question are appropriate for different purposes. The moderator should be aware of the options available and skilled at rapidly selecting the most suitable format and formulating the wording accordingly. Here are some of the choices:

Open questions: those that start with 'what', 'why', 'when', 'where', 'who' or 'how', or phrases that imply the need for more than yes/no answers (most of the moderator's questions will be of this type);

Clarifying questions: for example 'was that before or after you told your manager you weren't interested?'; or 'is that everyone's experience?';

Non directive prompts: a simple 'uhuh', 'yes' or 'I see, do go on', or even a pleasantly expectant silence, may be all that is required to encourage the free flow of ideas. However, excessive prompting can be distracting;

The probe: the successive use of probe questions, looking for further detail or evidence or more specific information, will lead to discussion being funnelled into narrower and narrower areas. However, if used excessively, probe questions can make people feel as if they are being interrogated.

THE CONSTRUCTIVE CHALLENGE

At times it may be necessary to question the opinions expressed in order to encourage participants to think more carefully about the issue and/or ensure that all views have been explored. This must be timed carefully so as not to lose rapport with the group and used in such a way that it does not suggest that the moderator is personally aligned with some opposing viewpoint.

QUESTIONS TO AVOID

Double negatives: for example, 'What improvements will not be brought about by relocating to Apsley?';

Leading questions: for example, 'Given the amount of time and effort put into this initiative, do you agree that it shows that the company cares about you?';

Multiple questions: for example, 'What do you think about the clarity of the briefing and the route by which it reached you?';

Embroidered questions (often brought about by nervousness): for example, 'What do you think about the company? Do you think we can do it? ... I mean, is it alright?';

Statements posing as questions: for example, Don't you think it would be a good idea to...?'.

LISTENING TECHNIQUES

The focus group moderator and scribe should listen actively and noticeably to what the group is saying because:

- it demonstrates that they value the group's views;

- the moderator bases subsequent questions upon earlier answers from participants;

- they both need to come away from the focus group with a complete impression of the views expressed, and be able to report these accurately.

Active listening involves attending to more than the literal meaning of what is stated. Moderators and scribes should attend to other features that may be just as important as the surface content, and be ready to follow them up in their questioning, for example:

underlying assumptions: implicit in what the participants are saying, but not actually expressed;
body language: nodding in agreement, looking at the speaker for reassurance, other non-verbal signals, such as tone of voice;
gaps and hesitations.

Active listening involves entering into the mind of the speaker; trying to understand the speaker's construction of reality without making a judgement about its validity.

The following techniques can be helpful in demonstrating that you are indeed listening in this way (although used carelessly they can have the opposite effect):

non-verbal signals: nodding, posture and eye contact indicate to the speaker that they have your attention and encourage them to continue;
summarise verbally what the speaker has said: to check understanding and demonstrate listening;
express empathy: comments that indicate comprehension and appreciation of the speaker's perceptions of the situation (not the same as agreeing with the speaker or showing sympathy, which may undermine impartiality and/or fuel the speaker's emotions).

MANAGING PROBLEMS

A group of eight people contains up to 28 independent lines of communication; clearly, even a small group has the potential to become unmanageably complex. One of the primary responsibilities of the moderator is to ensure that the group becomes and remains productive and does not run out of control. Some of the problems that may arise at one time or another are described below.

DESTRUCTIVE GROUPS

Groups have the potential to enter a destructive spiral, particularly when discussing an emotive topic. One negative comment can lead to another and another and another, with each participant echoing and reinforcing the previous comments.

When this happens, the moderator needs to take the lead in raising the tone of the discussion. Gentle but persistent nudging should be the first tactic, using phrases such as:

- 'Yes, things do sound bleak, but can you think of any benefits at all?';

- 'So we've heard how bad things are; what steps would you take to improve the situation?';

- 'What can we learn from this experience?';

- 'How can we stop this happening again?';

- 'What would look good for you?'.

One strategy is to shift to another topic or task in the hope that this will break the destructive rhythm. Another is to structure the discussion so that participants are forced to consider positive as well as negative aspects of the situation, by, for example, asking them to list pros and cons separately.

If people keep returning to the same negative issues, it may be necessary to remind them that the ground has already been covered, and that the group needs to consider other things. Accurately recording concerns, perhaps by listing them on an 'Issues Board', may reassure participants that their adverse comments have been recorded, and free them to move on to new areas.

UNPARTICIPATIVE GROUPS

When a group is unresponsive, give it time. The chances are that sooner or later people will start to get involved.

The moderator should be prepared to warm things up gradually and not to force the pace. Begin with simple, clear, open questions that are relevant to everyone's experience and put aside the more complex issues for later.

It may be worthwhile to spend some time on topics unrelated to the research in order to get people talking (for example, the weather, current work activities, travel arrangements). Share some of your own experience as a demonstration that it is 'OK' to be open.

Criticizing the group for its failure to respond may cause resentment, so the moderator should:

- try to adopt a style that is gently encouraging without being inquisitorial; use open gestures;

- consider moving closer to the group (in a manner that is non-threatening);

- leave plenty of space between questions, giving

people time to respond or react enthusiastically to any contributions that are made;

- bring in others by throwing individual comments open to the group; for example, 'How does everyone else feel about that?'.

Some groups will inevitably be less outgoing and harder work than others, but if the lack of participation is extreme and persists for a long time it may be worth probing to see if there is some underlying reason.

DIGRESSING GROUPS

Although the moderator is generally concerned with getting the participants to talk freely, sometimes the flow has to be stopped or diverted when too much time is spent on issues far removed from the purposes of the research. This may not be easy to do without upsetting the group members, but an attempt could be made by saying: 'Shall we come back to that later, after I have finished my questions?'.

ARGUMENTATIVE GROUPS

Particularly during periods when people are under pressure, some groups may repeatedly and aggressively challenge the moderator to respond to their concerns. Typically from 'headquarters', the moderator can be perceived to represent authority and hence become a focus for employee dissatisfaction.

While noting and responding to any immediate issues, the moderator must avoid becoming embroiled in a debate with the group. It may help to acknowledge the participants' frustration at not having someone respond to their anxieties, and the moderator should explain to the group how important it is for them to maintain the role of a neutral collector and reporter of opinions.

Be aware that by siding too much with the group, the moderator can become trapped in the unofficial role of employee champion, which again could undermine the credibility of the research.

MANAGING DIFFICULT INDIVIDUALS

The legitimate expert
The presence of a legitimate expert among a group of novices may have an inhibiting effect on the discussion. Screening during the recruitment phase may help to eliminate the problem but, should experts appear nevertheless, it may be best to co-opt them and, for example, ask them to withhold their opinions, but bring them in from time to time to clarify matters of fact.

The self appointed expert
Such 'experts' seldom have genuine expertise, but may offer their opinions as fact and to intimidate other members of the group. The moderator can combat this by making it clear that the views of all members of the group are of interest. If the 'expert' continues to dominate the discussion, the moderator may need to use more assertive techniques such as displaying disinterest, avoiding eye contact and even cutting the speaker off in mid-sentence.

Friends
As far as possible, having friends or close work colleagues in the same group should be avoided. If this is not possible, the moderator will need to ensure that they do not engage in private conversations to the exclusion of other members of the group, and that they do not reinforce one another's

views to the extent that it creates an imbalance of opinion within the group.

Hostile group members

Even the most hostile participants may become more co-operative once their initial suspicions have been allayed. The moderator will need to show patience and tact in dealing with such individuals and be prepared to spend time addressing their concerns.

However, there comes a point at which the amount of effort involved in dealing with an aggressive or destructive participant is out of proportion to the likely gains, and threatens to undermine the group. In such circumstances it may be necessary to give the offending person the option of leaving. To avoid embarrassment the request could be made privately during a brief recess.

Reticent individuals

It is not uncommon to find one or two participants in a group who are reluctant, through shyness, to join in. The technique here is to identify such individuals early, and create opportunities for them to contribute, without embarrassing them or making them feel uncomfortable. At least initially, invite them to comment on areas where you feel certain they will have something to say, perhaps factual rather than descriptive.

Attempts to include them must be made in a non threatening manner. Avoid wording such as 'Dave, we haven't heard much from you. Surely you have an opinion on this?'. This may be construed as offensive and lead to further withdrawal from the group. Above all, when the reticent members do finally contribute, the moderator must be sure to reinforce this through verbal and non verbal encouragement.

Confidential Plans

Testing people's reactions to policies that are merely under consideration, have yet to be agreed with trades unions, or are share price sensitive can pose a particular problem for focus groups. The dangers are that news of a proposal will leak before it has been properly agreed and/or that tentative proposals will be interpreted as having been decided already.

The moderator can emphasise the confidential or undecided nature of the proposals being considered, and it might even be possible to disguise genuine proposals by burying them among other bogus items. However, it is inevitable that participants will use the questions asked to speculate about the company's intentions and that they will share these predictions with colleagues.

Embarrassing Subjects

Work-based focus groups only seldom require people to discuss issues of a personal or sensitive nature, but there are occasions when these can arise (in the area of discipline or occupational health for example). Moderators need to anticipate when participants might find it awkward to share opinions or experiences in front of colleagues, and be sensitive to signs that this is happening.

Ensuring that the members of the group are strangers to one another can help people to open up on sensitive issues. Beginning with the less invasive questions, before leading gradually into the more delicate areas, gives people a chance to settle down and learn to trust each other before being asked to disclose more personal information. Another step that may help people to feel more secure is to obtain a verbal undertaking that group members will not disclose the content of the discussion outside the room.

The moderator can help to break the ice on difficult issues by talking openly about them. Signs of embarrassment will almost certainly encourage a similar response from participants. Allowing people to report on the experiences of friends and colleagues rather than from their own first hand knowledge is another useful tactic for enabling them to discuss sensitive topics without feeling embarrassed.

Finally, there may be some issues that are simply too personal for people to discuss in a forum of this type and for which alternative methods of data collection should be considered.

THE FINDINGS

WRITING THE REPORT

The client for the research project will require a written summary of the findings from the focus groups.

The report writer will, preferably, have conducted all the focus groups personally and will work from notes taken at the time. As a minimum, the person writing the report will have attended some of the group sessions to obtain a flavour of the views expressed. If working from secondary material provided by other people, the report writer should involve those who collected the raw data in the analysis process.

The research organiser will usually be responsible for the final shaping and finishing of the report, in order to ensure a consistent style and coherent content.

ANALYSIS

Quantitative data, such as grade and gender breakdowns, and polls among participants, can be collated and/or averaged across groups (for example, the numbers of people agreeing with a particular premise) and presented in the form of tables or graphs.

The descriptive material is less straightforward to handle. One approach is to condense what people have said by grouping specific comments under broad headings or 'themes'. For example, in response to the prompt 'What do people get out of working with the organisation?', themes might include 'satisfaction with the work', 'financial rewards' and 'social contact'. It may be helpful to identify broad themes in a group exercise.

Having identified relevant themes, a feel for the relative importance of each can be gained by counting the number of times comments related to each theme occur in the record of the discussion.

At the same time the report writer will need to be vigilant in capturing ideas and connections between themes even though they may not be particularly frequent. One advantage of the focus group method is that it permits unexpected or creative ideas to emerge and be reported back to the client, even where these do not represent the majority opinion.

STRUCTURE

The order and emphasis of the report may be dictated by

- the structure of the focus group itself;

- the initial brief provided by the client;

- a theoretical perspective chosen to help make sense of the findings.

Where the focus group structure was initially defined only loosely, a suitable structure for the report may be apparent from the flow of the discussions and the themes that emerge.

It is advisable to anticipate and overcome any obvious questions or objections that the client might raise in response to the findings, as these could easily divert attention from the important issues.

The inclusion of 'signposts', such as contents page, headings and sub-headings, will help readers find their way around the report.

A typical report will include the following sections:

- executive summary;

- background;

- research objectives;

- methodology;

- findings;

- interpretation/discussion;

- recommendations;

- appendices containing data tables (for reporting quantitative data).

REPORTING QUALITATIVE DATA

Reporting on focus groups provides an opportunity to bring the findings alive by illustrating them with verbatim comments. These should be relatively brief and used sparingly for maximum impact. Nothing should be reported that would enable an individual to be identified by name or implication.

Minority views can be included, but need to be clearly labelled as such. Above all, the report should aim to provide a balanced, accurate and objective summary of the opinions expressed by participants. There is no point in including gratuitously offensive material, but neither is there advantage in presenting a grossly watered down version of events.

The best reports will give the reader a condensed, but objective and realistic account of what it would have been like to observe the groups in action, plus a framework for making sense of the views expressed, and a way forward for responding to them.

COMMON MISTAKES

The following errors could easily undermine the impact of the report:

Poor spelling/grammar/layout
The reader equates this with a lack professionalism.

Report too long
There is only so much that a busy client, however interested, is prepared to read, so keep the report short and include a brief opening summary of the key findings.

Excessive detail

Excessive detail in any part of the report can easily obscure the important issues, leaving the reader unable to 'see the wood for the trees'. Pick out the points of most interest and relevance and be prepared to lose some information in the process. If you feel that some material might be wasted by not being included, offer the client the option of coming back to you for further detail on specific issues.

Factual errors

Mistakes about the client, the work area or the organisation may cast doubt upon the quality of the researcher's work. Bear in mind that the situation may well have changed since the project was first discussed and get an update before presenting the conclusions.

To report inaccurate perceptions held by group participants is not, of course, an error of fact by the report writer. Even so, it may be worth acknowledging, for the satisfaction of the client, that the views held appear to be based on misinformation.

Unconventional style

The writing style should be impartial and understated, with the author playing no part in the proceedings. Emotive language should be avoided as it can undermine the perceived objectivity of the report. Be cool and dispassionate and let the facts speak for themselves.

Over-interpretation

Explanations for the attitudes reported can be of great help to the client in understanding how best to respond. However, avoid parading pet theories that cannot be supported by the data as this will undermine your credibility. Make clear whether your explanation is tentative and being floated for discussion purposes only, or whether it is compulsive and overwhelmingly supported by the data. If the latter, be sure that you have evidence to refute any rival explanations.

Over-prescriptive

Be clear about the extent to which you are expected to suggest further steps. Remember that the client may well have superior knowledge and may have spent more time thinking about the available options than you have. Your client is likely to resent being told how to do his or her job, and will have greater commitment to solutions developed personally.

Glib solutions

Where you are expected to make recommendations, beware of reaching for the easy solution, such as 'set up a working party'; run a training programme; 'spend more money on X, Y or Z'. Few real life situations are this straightforward.

If the solution seems obvious, consider why no one appears to have done it already and whether there may be undesirable side effects. Indicate that you are aware of the drawbacks of each proposal as well as the benefits.

FEEDBACK TO PARTICIPANTS

It is important that all participants be given some form of feedback, within a reasonable period (usually three to four weeks after taking part). The feedback should be provided on a personal basis; not through an inappropriate channel such as the company newspaper .

Feedback is necessary because:

- it is a common courtesy to those who have

voluntarily given time and effort to taking part;

- the promise of feedback encourages interest at the time of the event and therefore must be honoured;

- it demonstrates that participants' opinions have been taken seriously, thus increasing involvement and shared ownership of issues;

- people are more inclined to take part in subsequent research programmes if they feel that their past involvement has made a difference.

Agree the mechanisms for feedback with the client in advance, ensure that moderators fully understand these arrangements, and communicate them to participants. Avoid unrealistic undertakings to participants about what feedback to expect and when (for example, that all data will be provided, irrespective of its commercial sensitivity).

For most focus group participants, the preferred method for feedback (and also the most difficult to organize) is direct and face-to-face contact. Alternatively, a letter should be sent to each participant by the moderator, the research project manager or, preferably, the research client. It should be positive and sincere, and must include the following:

- appreciation for the participant's contribution;

- a summary of the main findings (accurately reflecting and accepting the concerns raised at the groups);

- information on how the findings are being used and what actions are likely to result.

In addition it may be appropriate to include:

- a contact point for queries;

- a facility to obtain more information;

- an invitation to submit additional comments to the client.

WIDER FEEDBACK

At the planning stage it should have been agreed with the client whether a summary of the main findings should be provided to a wider audience in the organisation, or beyond, and how this will be achieved. Many people other than the participants may be aware of the research and anticipate hearing about the outcome.

Changes implemented later as a result of the research may be relevant and interesting to some who are not even aware that focus groups have taken place.

The group moderators, scribes and organisers may also have a special interest in the eventual outcomes. Again, this communication should have been planned in advance, and agreed with the client.

USE OF THE FINDINGS

As with all research, the steps between presenting the results and bringing about appropriate action are the hardest to complete. Unfortunately, too much excellent research continues to end up in someone's bottom drawer.

To avoid this, a process for discussing and working with the results should be agreed in advance with the client and other stakeholders. If the research is credible, well presented and meets the client's needs, it is more likely to result in significant action. A skilfully handled workshop or feedback session may be useful to explore resistance and secure the necessary commitment.

Finally, the research, although obtained with a particular purpose and client in mind, may also be relevant elsewhere in the organisation. A useful approach is to identify such links and, with the client's permission, draw the findings to the attention of appropriate people. A small steering group could carry out this task.

REVIEW OF THE RESEARCH

Good practice in project management recommends that projects of all types should be reviewed on completion.

Unfortunately, much focus group research is not reviewed in this way. In some cases this may be because people are too busy concentrating on the information gathered rather than the process by which it was obtained. Alternatively, particularly after a prolonged data collection exercise, it may be that fatigue sets in and interest in the project wanes.

BENEFITS OF A REVIEW

A review does not have to be a large-scale exercise and, in fact, it makes sense that the time and effort spent on it should not outweigh the possible benefits.

Besides identifying learning points, a review has the following side benefits:

- it reduces the risk of overlooking something that may have undesirable consequences if left unactioned;

- it demonstrates the seriousness of meeting the client's needs;

- it shows others in the company that you are committed to continuous improvement;

- it may reveal deficiencies which are possible to remedy;

- it has a symbolic value, marking the end of the project and psychologically 'freeing' people to move on to new activities;

- involvement in the review may encourage the client to reconsider the research findings and initiate additional action;

VALIDATION

Validation is primarily about checking the extent to which the research met its overall objectives. Clearly, the more accurately objectives and associated success measures were defined at the outset, the easier it will be to demonstrate whether or not they have been achieved.

Although there may be some 'hard measures' available (such as information on whether or not deliverables were produced as specified), much of the review will depend on the perceptions of various stakeholders, each of whom might view the situation differently. The person carrying out the validation might therefore want to collect these views systematically before arriving at any conclusions.

Since people's reactions may depend on when they are tested in relation to the events concerned, it is important to consider when the validation should take place. Some benefits may take time to come to fruition, while favourable reactions may fade after an initial period of euphoria. If there are any shortcomings in the outcomes of the project, a closer look at the process may help to identify where things went wrong.

EVALUATION

It is important to evaluate whether the project was worthwhile. Were the gains sufficient to justify the time and effort put in?

Some costs and benefits, such as staff costs, will be quantifiable, whereas others, such as improved morale and productivity, will be harder to determine in many instances. Despite the difficulties, a complete evaluation of the research should include a systematic appraisal of the costs and benefits involved.

The research manager or, better still, an independent third party will need to synthesize and summarise the views expressed and the recommendations for improvement.

Typically, the research manager and the client will then hold a joint session to examine the findings and see what changes they can implement. To learn from the experience, both will need to be open to criticism as well as praise.

Finally, the recommendations need to be drawn to the attention of any others who are able to deliver the improvements suggested.

USEFUL
INFORMATION

This checklist will help you to ensure that you cover the many different areas involved in organising focus group research. Although it is intended to be fairly comprehensive, not all steps will be relevant to all situations. Additional actions may be required in certain circumstances.

INITIAL PLANNING

Activity	*By Whom*	*By When*
Prepare client brief		
Agree methodology		
Prepare research proposal		
Carry out desk research		
Check research library		
Define success measurement		
Agree client involvement		
Check fit with research year plan		
Clear project with research co-ordination group		

CONTROL

Activity	By Whom	By When
Milestones		
Work breakdown		
Schedule activity		
Updates to client		
Progress meetings		
Project documentation		

PRE-PUBLICITY

Activity	By Whom	By When
Draft communications plan		
Pre launch publicity		

VENUES

Activity	By Whom	By When
Decide locations		
Book venues		
Arrange catering		
Check arrangements for furniture		
Arrange the provision of equipment		
Ascertain transport arrangements		
Arrange access to buildings		

PARTICIPANTS

Activity	By Whom	By When
Agree sample size and base		
Obtain names and contact details for participants		
Brief contact resource		
Recruit participants		
Send out call up papers		
Arrange contact point		
Regularly monitor the success of participant recruitment		
Arrange release of participants with their managers		

FOCUS GROUP DESIGN

Activity	By Whom	By When
Design outline of focus group		
Add detail to the outline		
Test focus group design		
Revise focus group design following the test		
Validate focus group design with client		
Revise design after each focus group (if applicable)		

RESEARCHERS (MODERATORS, SCRIBES, ETC)

Activity	By Whom	By When
Select and book researchers		
Brief and train researchers		
Arrange and run practice sessions		
Set standards		
Run focus groups		

ANALYSIS

Activity	By Whom	By When
Collate outputs from focus groups		
Organise data from focus groups		
Summarise findings		
Interpret findings		
Write summary report		
Prepare presentation of findings		

FEEDBACK

Activity	By Whom	By When
Feedback findings to client		
Feedback findings to participants		
Feedback findings to researchers		
Feedback findings to project organisers		
Feedback findings to others in organisation		
Feedback details of improvements to participants		
Feedback details of improvements to researchers		
Feedback details of improvements to project organisers		
Feedback details of improvements to others in the organisation		
Submit findings to data library		

ACTION PLANNING

Activity	By Whom	By When
Agree approach		
Determine causes		
Identify steps and processes		
Plan implementation		
Monitor progress		
Measure effects		
Review plans		

REVIEW

Activity	By Whom	By When
Review processes		
Review outputs		
Identify improvement actions		

APPENDIX 1

Viewpoint BT Case Study 1
THE EMPLOYEE HANDBOOK

BT's central personnel function wanted to introduce an employee handbook that would contain information on terms and conditions of employment, and on the personnel policies and processes that apply to them.

Viewpoint BT, the company wide programme of focus groups, was used to test the concept. People were asked what they thought of the idea and were presented with some mock-ups to examine and comment on. Among the points made were suggestions that the document should be simple, compact and coherent, and should list further information sources. People also felt that the information would need to be updated on a regular basis.

Some months after the first edition was issued, it was again tested at *Viewpoint BT* focus groups. It had been agreed that the handbook would be reissued annually and feedback on the first edition was needed prior to commencing work on the second. The client commented: '... it was satisfying to see that much of the feedback was positive, as we had tried to tailor the development of the booklet to the feedback we had received from earlier focus groups...'.

Particular note was taken of the fact that the information was useful for reference purposes; that there were areas of duplication; and that a filofax or binder format would be preferred by some people.

The focus groups provided detailed comments and feedback that would have been difficult to obtain through any other method.

APPENDIX 2

Viewpoint BT Case Study 2
FURTHER INVESTIGATION OF EMPLOYEE ATTITUDE DATA

BT conducts an annual employee attitude survey (CARE), which asks BT people for their views on a range of subjects, including what they think about their managers, their working environment and the development and training they receive.

Each year, after the questionnaires have been completed and returned, the CARE team runs a series of focus groups to gather people's views on the implementation of the survey and on the company wide results. This enables the team to review the way in which the survey was processed, to review the contents of the survey itself and also to develop an understanding of the issues behind the results.

In 1995 much of the focus group feedback indicated that people felt the questionnaire had taken too long to complete and was too complex. In addition, participants were asked to give their own views of the CARE Survey results and to suggest, with specific examples, what action BT would take to make improvements in those areas which needed them. The data gathered from the focus groups helped the BT Board understand the issues at a more individual level, adding depth to the numerical data provided by the survey. This, along with feedback from key stakeholders, resulted in a shorter and simpler 1996 version of the CARE Survey.

APPENDIX 3

Viewpoint BT Case Study 3
EMPLOYEES' EVENING

BT held an Employees' Evening in Newcastle on 17 July 1996. Focus groups were used to assist in preparing for this event.

Viewpoint BT, the company wide programme of focus groups, was used beforehand to develop a clearer understanding of:

- the key issues and concerns, both good and bad, for BT people;

- any functional, geographic or manager/non-manager differences in relation to these issues and concerns;

- the topics that were likely to be raised at the Employees' Evening.

The information gained from the focus groups gave an idea of the local issues and the strength of feeling behind them. It was put together as briefing material for the panellists at the Newcastle Employees' Evening, enabling them to prepare constructive replies to topics that were likely to be raised.

The participants at the focus groups were also asked: 'If you had one question for Sir Peter Bonfield, what would it be?'. The responses provided useful material for Sir Peter's opening address and helped him focus on issues that had been identified as important.